PUBLIC EXPENDITURE AND THE SELECT COMMITTEES OF THE COMMONS

This book is to be returned on or before
the last date stamped below

PLYMOUTH POLYTECHNIC
LEARNING RESOURCES CENTRE
Telephone: (0752) 221312 ext: 5413
(After 5p.m. (0752) 264661 weekdays only)

This book is subject to recall if required by another reader.
Books may be renewed by phone, please quote Telepen number.
CHARGES WILL BE MADE FOR OVERDUE BOOKS

Public Expenditure and the Select Committees of the Commons

VILMA FLEGMANN

Gower

Published by

Gower Publishing Company Limited
Gower House,
Croft Road,
Aldershot,
Hants   GU11 3HR
England

Gower Publishing Company,
Old Post Road,
Brookfield,
Vermont 05036
U S A

British Library Cataloguing in Publication Data

Flegmann, Vilma
  Public expenditure and the select committees of
  the Commons.
  1. Great Britain, *Parliament* ——Committees
  2. Great Britain——Appropriations and expenditures
  I. Title
  336.3'9'0941   HJ2096

ISBN: 0 566 05013 7

Printed in Great Britain by Paradigm Print,
Gateshead, Tyne & Wear

Contents

Acknowledgements

I wish to thank the Leverhulme Trust for their generous support for the research on which this book is based.

I am grateful to those Members of Parliament who gave up some of their time to talk to me about their work on select committees and to the senior civil servants whose interest in the project and willingness to discuss it I wish to place on record. The study could not have been carried out without their co-operation.

To all select committees I owe thanks for the many interesting hours spent at their meetings.

I am indebted to the Rt. Hon Lord Barnett for reading and commenting on the manuscript and to Professor Cedric Sandford for his interest in the project and his comments on the final draft.

My thanks are also due to Karen Messer for careful typing of the manuscript.

To my family, once again, my gratitude for their good humoured tolerance of my preoccupation with matters of 'the public purse'.

Vilma Flegmann

Introduction

Over a century ago Walter Bagehot remarked on the "exceptional disability" [1] of the House of Commons in financial matters. Bagehot did not regard this disability as a threat to effective parliamentary government, since he believed that finance should be the concern of Cabinet only and he was also convinced that the House of Commons had no interest in economies and had a greater tendency to profiligacy than any Minister of the day.

Is the House of Commons of the 1980s better equipped or more interested in the consideration of 'sordid financial matters' than it was in the days of Bagehot?

In an attempt to answer this question, this book examines recent developments in parliamentary procedures: the establishment of a new comprehensive select committee system in 1979 for the improved monitoring of expenditure, policy and administration of the major government departments.

The book considers the way in which the committees carried out their task with respect to the examination of departmental expenditure during the first Parliament after their appointment and is based on a two year study which has included documentary analysis, attendance at committee meetings and an extensive interview programme in Westminster and Whitehall.

The study was undertaken after some early indications that the monitoring of expenditure did not appear to be the major item on most committees' agenda, even though it was expected and hoped that it would be.

The book is in three parts.

Part I   discusses the role of select committees in the control of public expenditure and the background to the 1979 reform;

Part II   analyses the work of the committees since 1979, and considers the views in Westminster and Whitehall on the impact of the committees' work;

Part III assesses the work of the committees and suggests some changes which would enable them to become more effective instruments for the parliamentary scrutiny of public expenditure.

While the book draws heavily on the variety of views expressed to the author during the period of the study in Westminster and Whitehall, and on extensive discussions with academic colleagues both in this country and overseas, the conclusions are the sole responsibility of the author.

NOTES

[1] Bagehot, W. The English Constitution, 11th Impression. Fontana 1975. p. 154.

PART I

1 The constitutional role of select committees in the control of public expenditure

The constitutional position of Parliament [1] in relation to government finance has changed little since the days of Bagehot. Government, representing the Crown, initiates expenditure, the Commons grant it and the Lords assent to the grant.

The framework of financial control to be exercised by the House of Commons has also remained essentially unchanged:
1. approval of Government policies with their
   contingent financial liabilities;
2. granting of finance to carry out the Government's
   programme;
3. scrutiny of the Government's performance.

Although the constitutional framework has remained unchanged, the past 100 years have witnessed a gradual, and in the last two decades an accelerated resurgence of interest in financial matters in the House of Commons. Much of this interest was the direct result of the rapid increase in the involvement of the state in the economic activities of the country following the Second World War.

The establishment of the welfare state together with the post-war nationalisation programme resulted in the public sector becoming the major single provider of employment. In the civil service alone employment increased by 52 per cent in the number of non-industrial civil servants and by 94 per cent in the number of industrial civil servants between 1938 and 1950. [2]

In 1938 the public sector provided 9.9 per cent of all employment, by 1950 this increased to 24.4 per cent [3] and by 1982 even further to 33 per cent. [4]

Governments had also become the major spenders of the countries resources. Public expenditure as a per centage of national income increased from the prewar 30 per cent of GNP in 1938 [5] to 50.8 per cent GDP in 1975. [6]

It was inevitable that Parliament which achieved its supremacy through the control of finance would renew its interests in such matters, when Government finance began to affect more and more of the life of the electorate. No longer was Parliament representing the interests of the tax-payers only; MPs became representatives of public sector employees, of the consumers of publicly provided goods and services, and of the recipients of an increasing range of benefits.

The traditional role of Parliament in controlling Government finance under the new circumstances needed to be re-examined.

The pressure for such re-examination received further impetus from the changes which took place in the composition of the House of Commons after the war. Increasingly, Members of Parliament entered political life after a university education, frequently from occupations which could not be easily combined with a parliamentary career, thus becoming full-time MPs with time on their hands and skills at their disposal to take part in detailed work through the committees of the House. Table 1 shows the changing educational background of MPs from the two major political parties between 1935 and 1983.

Traditionally, the two of the major roles of financial control by the House of Commons, the approval of Government policies, and the granting of Supply were carried out largely on the floor of the House while detailed scrutiny of the Government's performance was conducted through the select committee system, mainly by the Committee of Public Accounts.

The Committee of Public Accounts, (PAC) established by Gladstone in 1861 examine Government Departments annually, on the basis of their accounts audited by the Comptroller and Auditor General. The PAC's scrutiny is essentially ex post and their order of reference does not include the examination of how public funds are allocated. [7]

Table 1 Educational Background of MPs

Year	Percentage of MPs with a university education	
	Conservative	Labour
1935	57	19
1945	58	32
1964	63	46
1974 Oct	69	57
1979*	75	61
1983**	72	58

Source: D. Butler & A. Sloman: British Political Facts
         1900-1975, p.155.

*   The Times Guide to the House of Commons 1979, p.281.

** The Times Guide to the House of Commons 1983 (data
    tabulated by the Author).

Since 1912, intermittently, the House of Commons has also
appointed Estimates Committees, to examine particular estimates
and consider how the policies implied in them could be carried
out more economically. [8] Though their functions were much
less clearly defined than those of the PAC, in the early years
following the 'public expenditure explosion' they were still
considered to provide "...ample scope" [9] for parliamentary
control.

Executive control of public expenditure was, however,
receiving renewed attention. In 1959 the Government appointed
a committee under the chairmanship of Lord Plowden to consider
the theory and practice of Treasury control of public
expenditure and to suggest solutions for the common problems of
all Governments, "...how to bring growth of public expenditure
under better control and how to contain it within such limits
as the Government think desirable". [10] In their report, the
Plowden Committee recommended regular and systematic surveys of
public expenditure as a whole over a period of years in
relation to prospective resources, greater attention to
improving management throughout the public sector and
opportunities for constructive parliamentary control. In
response to the Plowden recommendations, the Public Expenditure
Survey Committee (PESC) was introduced in 1961 and, after a
considerably longer period of gestation, the first public
expenditure white paper was published in December 1969

out-lining the Government's expenditure plans for the coming years.

The measures introduced to improve the planning, allocation and management of public expenditure by the Executive necessitated the review of parliamentary machinery available for scrutinizing government finance. The Estimates Committee was regarded by many as inadequate for scrutinizing Estimates effectively for some time. Einzig suggested that after World War II, they gave up even the pretence of dealing with the Estimates. [11]

The Select Committee of Procedure in their report on "Scrutiny of Public Expenditure and Administration" in 1969 [12] therefore recommended that the Estimates Committee should be replaced by a Select Committee on Expenditure with wider terms of reference more appropriate to the needs:
1) to provide information on the planning of public expenditure,
2) to scrutinize Government decisions on plans and priorities and
3) check on their execution by the Departments.

In response to the recommendations of the Procedure Committee the Expenditure Committee was appointed in 1970, with terms of reference considerably extended beyond that of its predecessor. They were given the powers to examine longer term issues of expenditure policy as well as current implementation of departmental programmes, "and to consider any papers on public expenditure presented to the House and such Estimates as may seem fit to the committee". [13] A significant new principle was thus established for Parliament to take an active interest in the consideration of the whole field of public expenditure, not only those related to the two-thirds which was covered by the Supply Estimates.

The new committee, with a larger membership than the Estimates Committee, was to operate through a system of sub-committees and was expected to provide a co-ordinated and reasonably even coverage of all areas of public expenditure. In addition to the traditional duties of scrutinizing committees, outlined by the Haldene Report as early as in 1918, "... to secure continuous and well informed interest...in the execution...of the policy which Parliament has laid down..." [14] the Expenditure Committee was expected to fulfil some further functions.
Concern over the balance of power between the Legislature and the Executive has been a recurrent theme of British constitutional history, and attempts to 'control' the Executive

have long been bound-up with the control of expenditure. Originally intended to safeguard the constitution against an excessive build up of military force by the Crown in peacetime, control of the purse-string has always been regarded as the most important role for Parliament in controlling the Executive. Increasing Executive power had unquestionably become a genuine concern both inside and outside Parliament and the new select committee was expected to make a real contribution towards establishing a more acceptable balance of power, away from what later Lord Hailsham described as an 'elective dictatorship'. [15]

Within the traditional framework the House could exercise financial control either during the consideration of the financial aspects of policy proposals or in scrutinzing the performance of Governments.

The new Expenditure Committee was to assist the House in carrying out these duties and in addition was expected to provide new channels for communication between Government, Parliament and various interest groups. The wider range of information obtained through the committee investigations was to lead to better informed policy formulation and to more effective policy implementation.

The Committee was provided with more generous facilities than its predecessor - expert advisers, some research assistance, and the facility to make visits outside Parliament both at home and abroad. They were authorized to call on a wider range of witnesses including Government Ministers, although by no means without restrictions.

The work of the sub-committees was to be co-ordinated by the General Sub-Committee but, in fact, each tended to operate as individual committees. From amongst the multifarious range of possible topics each chose those which appeared to be of the greatest interest to the chairman or to the most forceful members of the sub-committee. Control of public expenditure, or the consideration of particular Estimates, hardly ever turned out to be the focus of their interests. Their task was not made any easier by the inadequacy and irregularity of the information Governments provided for Parliament and the public about public expenditure. Public expenditure White Papers did not appear at regular times [16] and they provided information in a form which was at the same time both insufficient and difficult for MPs to use.

Gradually, the sub-committees developed their own profiles of interests, and usually continued work similar to that carried out by the Estimates Committee - examining expenditure on some particular project or programme. However, there was an increase in the number of inquiries which aimed to provide information for forthcoming policy debates or attempted to influence the shaping of new policies. The Expenditure Committee made some important contributions towards redressing the balance of power between the Legislature and the Executive through a series of well-researched reports which improved the standard of parliamentary and public debates, and drew attention to the shortcomings of the Government machinery from time to time. The Expenditure Committee also established select committees as a potential source of ideas for new policy formulation and a channel through which interest groups could bring their own proposals more directly to the notice of Parliament.

However, as the new instrument for more effective parliamentary scrutiny of Government finance, the Expenditure Committee proved to be ineffectual. Indeed, while public expenditure continued its seemingly inexorable upward march the sub-committees appeared to have virtually given up any attempts to 'examine longer terms issues of expenditure policy'. During the parliamentary session of '75-76, following the financial year when public expenditure overstepped the 50 per cent mark as a proportion of GDP, only the General Sub-Committee, the monitoring Sub-committee for overall public expenditure, conducted any inquiry into public expenditure.

The Queen's Speech in November 1975 announced a major review of parliamentary procedures and practices for the coming Session and Committees on Procedures were appointed in both Houses in the summer of 1976.

It was to be expected that such a review in the case of the House of Commons would include a critical examination of the procedures available for financial scrutiny, and not unexpected that the review would result in a report which drew attention to the shortcomings of the existing arrangements and put forward proposals for improvements.

True to expectations, when the House of Commons Select Committee on Procedure presented their report to the House in July 1978, [17] their recommendations included far-reaching and fundamental changes in the select committee structure to enable the House to provide improved scrutiny of all aspects of the Executive's actions.

NOTES

[1] In terms of financial control Parliament means the House of Commons, since the Parliament Act 1911 removed the last remaining rights of the House of Lords with respect to Money Bills.

[2] Butler & Sloman: British Political Facts 1900-1975, p.239.

[3] M. Abramowitz & V. Eliasberg: The Growth of Public Employment in Great Britain NBER 1957.

[4] Reply to Parliamentary Question, Hansard, Vol. 46, cl. 74 (19.7.1983).

[5] A.T. Peacock: The Political Economy of Public Spending (1971) Mercantile Credit Lecture, University of Reading, Nov. (1971).

[6] Reply to Parliamentary Question, Hansard Vol. 28, cl. 541-42, (28.7.1982).

[7] For a detailed examination of the work of the PAC, see FLEGMANN, V: Called to Account, Gower 1980

[8] ERSKINE MAY: Parliamentary Practice, 19th edition, p. 672.

[9] Control of Public Expenditure (The Plowden Report) Cmnd. 1432. 1961 p. 25.

[10] Plowden, op. cit. p.5.

[11] Einzig P. The Control of the Purse, Secker & Warburg 1959, Ch. 30.

[12] 1R Select Committee on Procedure 1968-69. HC 410.

[13] Standing Order No. 87.

[14] Haldene Report "Machinery of Government" Cd. 9230, p.225.

[15] Lord Hailsham: The Dilemma of Democracy, Collins 1978, p.9.

[16] Robinson, A. Parliament and Public Spending, Heinemann, 1978, p.91.

[17] 1st Report from the Select Committee on Procedure 1977-78, HC. 588.

2 The 1979 reform of the select committee system

The Procedure Committee recommended the "...reorganisation of the select committee structure to provide the House with the means of scrutinizing the activities of the public service on a continuing and systematic basis." [1] The report proposed that the Expenditure Committee and certain other select committees, namely the Select Committees on Science and Technology, on Nationalised Industries, on Overseas Development and on Race Relations should be replaced by a new, more extensive system of departmentally related select committees, each charged with the examination of all aspects of expenditure, policy and administration of a major Government department. "We hope that the new committees will concentrate much of their attention on the consideration of Estimates and other expenditure projections" [2] said the Report, but the Procedure Committee did not wish to impose any limitations on the freedom of the new committees to inquire into other, relevant matters. They recommended therefore that the terms of reference for the committees should be widely drawn and permissive rather than mandatory.

The 1978-79 Procedure Committee took considerably trouble to make detailed recommendations, much in excess of those which were put forward by earlier Procedure Committees which recommended select committee reforms. Their recommendations included proposals for staffing and accommodation as well as such fundamental issues as the speed of Government response to committee reports and increased debating opportunities in the House.

The House debated the report from the Procedure Committee in February 1979 [3] and there were strong pressures from both sides to implement the recommendations. Enthusiasm on the front-benches was muted. For the Conservatives, Norman St. John-Stevas undertook to "... present positive, constructive and helpful proposals based on this Report" [4] in the first Session of the new Parliament. On the Government side, the Lord President, Michael Foot expressed the view that "... it would be a great error for the House to proceed on the lines suggested by the Procedure Committee" [5] but bowing to pressure agreed to "... begin immediate consultations through the usual channels".

Following the 1979 General Election the incoming Conservative Government, with commendable speed, introduced the Motion for the appointment of twelve departmentally related select committees as a first stage of implementing the recommendations put forward by the 1977-78 Procedure Committee.

During the eleven hours debate on the Motion [6] the more than 50 MPs who took part made some grandiose claims for the occasion, calling it 'a most historic day', a 'crucial day', a 'turning point in constitutional history', yet the debate did in fact but cover much the same grounds as earlier debates heralding select committee reforms.

Introducing the Motion, the Leader of the House emphasised the high priority given to the review of the select committee system from the Procedure Committee's numerous recommendations. This was in recognition of the fact that "...while the power and effectiveness of Whitehall has grown, that of Westminster diminished". The new committee system was "... intended to redress the balance of power to enable the House of Commons to do more effectively the job it has been elected to do". [7] The reform was clearly also to benefit Parliament's somewhat tarnished reputation. "Parliament may not, for the moment, stand at the zenith of public esteem..." the Leader of the House conceded with admirable candour.

The loss of public esteem was attributed by Edward Du Cann, chairman of the powerful Public Accounts Committee until 1979, to Parliament's inability to "Control the purse strings. The crux of Parliament's progressive failure to control Whitehall... lies in its failure to control expenditure" [8]. Such a statement coming from a senior backbencher, who was also the first chairman of the Expenditure Committee, was a clear admission that the previous committee reforms failed to fulfil the expectations with respect to financial controls.

Although expenditure control as an important function for the new committee resurfaced time and again during the Debate, it was apparent that the major, historical change expected from the reform was 'to wrest the power from the Executive', and not only in financial matters.

Many of those taking part in the Debate sought in the new committees the effective means of controlling ministerial powers, prizing information out of secretive Governments as well as from departmental bureaucrats.

There were suggestions, both from long-established and younger Members, that in a large legislative assembly there was a need for alternative career opportunities for the "... ambitious, energetic and public spirited" able men and women [9] other than the front-benches.

There was even an ingenious suggestion from A. Duffy, a former chairman of the Expenditure Committee Trade and Industry Sub-Committee that "... select Committees can help Government by persuading Ministers to explain their actions and policies" [10].

The need to provide the new committees with all the necessary powers to carry out their work properly was emphasized by Sir Thomas Williams, who chaired the Procedure Committee inquiry. Sir Thomas also remarked that Governments are inclined to encourage the myth of Parliament as a "great forum of the nation", primarily a theatre, which it is not. Parliament is a "workshop" [11], with much of the work being carried out in the select committees.

Reservations about the proposals were largely on two grounds. Concern was expressed, similar to that voiced by Michael Foot as Lord President during the February Debate, about the committees encouraging consensus politics, reducing the importance of the floor of the House and "diminishing the scope for the general Member" [12] as the specialists from the committees took over. A further danger was foreseen in Departments 'hijacking' their committees [13] and using them to support their own aims and claims for funds.

The more cautious warned about making extravagant claims for the reform, important as it was, 'only time will tell how historic was this day' said C. Morris 'a first stage' noted J. Fookes.

Even the Leader of the House in his concluding speech emphasized that "the reform will not solve all our problems, but constitutes a decisive shift of the centre of power from Whitehall to Westminster" [14]. In general there was remarkably little opposition to the proposal. The 273 MPs who trooped through the Division Lobby at 1 o'clock in the morning on the 26 June 1979 to vote on the various Amendments gave their overwhelming support to the Government's Motion, and to the appointment of 12 departmentally related select committees under Standing Order. The abolition of the select committees on Expenditure, Race Relations, Overseas Development and the Nationalised Industries was agreed to.

The Order of Reference for the new committees stated that "Select committees shall be appointed to examine the expenditure, administration and policy of the principal government departments..." [15].

The order listed the names of the committees, the Departments they were to examine, their membership and quorum and the various powers the committees were to have in appointing sub-committees, sending for persons, papers and records, appointing advisers, adjourning from place to place and reporting to the House.

The twelve committees to be appointed were

      Agriculture
      Defence
      Education, Science & Arts
      Employment
      Energy
      Environment
      Foreign Affairs
      Home Affairs
      Industry & Trade
      Social Services
      Transport
      Treasury & Civil Service

The members of the new select committees were to be nominated by the Committee of Selection by a process "not widely known to other backbenchers" [16] and it was inevitable that for committees expected to redress the balance of power between the Executive and Legislature there was considerable sensitivity over the influence of the Whips' Office in nominating committee members. As a result it took more than five months of intricate negotiations before the departmental committees were finally nominated in November 1979. By this time, two further committees were added for the examination of the Welsh Office and the Scottish Office respectively following the rejection of the devolution proposal, thus bringing the number of departmental select committees to fourteen, and the number of backbenchers in the new select committees to 148. (The membership of the select committees abolished was 97). The chairmanship of the committees was divided between the two major parties with the Conservatives chairing Agriculture, Defence, Energy, Foreign Affairs, Home Affairs, Industry & Trade, Treasury & Civil Service and Labour chairing Education, Employment, Environment, Scottish Affairs, Social Services, Transport and Welsh Affairs.

A Liaison Committee was also appointed in January 1980, under Standing Order (SO.101) "to consider general matters relating to the work of the select committees and to give such advice on the work of the committees as might be sought by the House of Commons Commission." [17] The membership of the Liaison Committee includes most select committee chairmen and some chairmen of sub-committees as well. It is the role of the Liaison Committee to express joint views if and when necessary, co-ordinate the work of the committees to eliminate duplication of inquiries, and consider applications for foreign travel from select committees. More recently it has acquired [18] the important role of recommending which Estimates should be debated during Estimate Days.

Armed with their 'widely drawn and permissive' terms of reference, with support staff provided on a somewhat more generous level than for their predecessors and opportunities to engage outside advisers on an unrestricted scale, the new committees set out on their highly individual path to redress the balance of power between Executive and Legislature. Their interpretation of their role was much tempered by the exigencies of parliamentary politics, frequently diverted by the topical issues of the day.

NOTES

[1] 1R Select Cttee of Procedure, op. cit. p.cxxv.
[2] Ibid., p. iv.
[3] Hansard Vol. 962/3. 19-20 February 1979.
[4] Ibid., cl. 286.

[5] Ibid., cl. 383.
[6] Hansard Vol. 968/9. 26 June 1979.
[7] Hansard Vol. 968/9 cl. 35-36.
[8] Ibid. cl. 54-66.
[9] Hansard Vol. 968/9 cl. 156.
[10] Ibid. cl. 168
[11] Ibid. cl. 75.
[12] Hansard Vol. 968/9. cl. 178.
[13] Ibid., cl. 196
[14] Ibid., cl. 214.
[15] Ibid. cl. 249-252; later referred to as SO.99 (Erskine May, 20th Edition).
[16] Davies, A: Reformed Select Committees: The First Year, The Outer Circle Policy Unit 1980.
[17] Erskine May, 20th Edition, p. 1129.
[18] Under new procedures adopted in July 1982, 3 days in each session are allocated for the consideration of Estimates proposed by the Liaison Committee. New Standing Order 19.

PART II

3 Monitoring public expenditure — The work of the new committees during the first Parliamentary Session

The new committees which set to work in 1979 included an impressive proportion of experienced parliamentarians (there were 24 ex-ministers among the members) [1] but they were by no means well experienced in the scrutiny of public expenditure or departmental administration.

Half of the members had some previous select committee experience even if not necessarily as members of scrutinizing committees, and most of the chairmen had served on such committees, but the other half of the new team had no such background and included 30 new MPs who entered Parliament after the 1979 Election.

The programme for the committees thus had to be planned with a view to satisfying a variety of needs which were not always easily reconcilable. There was the need to embark on inquiries with sufficient political 'sex-appeal' to keep members interested and willing to devote the necessary time to committee work: to attend meetings and even prepare for them. Inquiries requiring the presence of Ministers as witnesses clearly came into this category, attracting publicity for the committee and providing the added satisfaction for individual backbenchers of being able to engage in dialogues with Ministers on a more or less equal footing. There are precious few opportunities for the newly arrived backbencher to address a direct question to a Cabinet Minister, declare that he (or she) finds the answer unsatisfactory and press on with further questions. Nor are long established backbenchers immune to the attractions of such opportunities. As a consequence, there was a heavy concentration on inquiries during the early years which required the evidence of ministerial witnesses, much in excess of the practices of earlier select committees. Between 1979 and 1982 there were 192 ministerial appearances in front of the new committees; [2] by contrast the Expenditure Committee had 7 ministers as witnesses between 1970 and 1974 [3] and the Select Committee on Nationalised Industries had 17 [4] during the last decade of their activities.

At the same time, there was a need to take on inquiries which were likely to result in 'useful' reports and 'useful' had long been accepted to imply agreed and if possible, unanimous reports. Inquiries which divide a committee strongly on party lines are unlikely to be concluded with unanimous reports.

The delicate balance which had to be maintained between vigorous, hard-pressing and publicity-worthy inquiries and objective, non-partisan reports was a major factor in deciding on the committees' programme.

The other major factor was the deliberately widely drawn terms of reference which, though intended to allow the committees freedom of choice, in fact placed far too many responsibilities on their shoulders.

Most of the committees, therefore, decided at the outset to focus their attention on certain aspects of the work of their departments, as they explained subsequently in their reports to the Liaison Committee in 1983. [5]

Only two of the committees, Agriculture and Defence said they were aiming to provide a balanced coverage of the EXPENDITURE, POLICY AND ADMINISTRATION of their departments and believed that they have partly succeeded. The majority made no such claims.

Policy inquiries held the centre of most committees' attention. This expressed itself either through major inquiries into long-term Government policies (Strategic Nuclear Weapons ; Depletion Policy on North Sea Oil ; Import and Export) or through inquiries aiming to influence current policy issues (New Immigration Rules; The New Training Initiative; Transfer of Heavy Vehicle Testing to the Private Sector.)

There was a strong and general desire to tackle topical

issues, and all committees carried out a number of short inquiries on some subjects of topical urgency. Some committees prided themselves on tackling controversial subjects (Environment, Home Affairs), others made a greater virtue of the unanimity of reports resulting from the judicious selection of subjects.

No committee regarded the examination of departmental expenditure as their most important role. Even those committees which claimed to have provided a balanced coverage devoted only a fraction of their time and energy to the consideration of Estimates. One evidence session per year on the Estimates or White Paper was not uncommon, and hardly ever were more than 3 out of the 30 - 40 annual meetings devoted to such matters.

Committees which examined expenditure plans for their departments with some regularity usually did so with the view of establishing the policy implications of general trends revealed in the expenditure figures. Sometimes committees did not find it necessary to present reports following their examination of Government Ministers about public expenditure plans. Defence, Education, Foreign Affairs, Scottish Affairs, all subscribed to this practice from time to time, which suggests that the committees were more interested in being informed about, than anxious to influence expenditure decisions.

All but two of the committees did make some attempt to give formal consideration to the Estimates or the Government's public expenditure plans relevant for their departments, as seen in Table 2. The exceptions were the Home Affairs and the Industry and Trade Committee, but for very different reasons. The Home Affairs Committee deliberately set out to become the 'eyes and ears of Parliament' and to provide briefing on current controversies or issues of topical political interests perhaps where legislative decision was pending. Expenditure scrutiny was peripheral to their purpose.

The Industry and Trade Committee on the other hand had an unusually wide field to cover and decided to provide continuous monitoring for some of the individual components of their public expenditure programme such as the British Steel Corporation, British Leyland, Concorde and the Post Office.

Indeed, most committees took an active interest in expenditure on some major project or programme within their department's budget and usually on a fairly continuous basis. Funding of the arts by the Education and Art Committee, Housing

Table 2. Select Committee Inquiries into Estimates and Public Expenditure Plans between 1979 and 1984

| Committee | Estimates | | PE White Paper |
	Main	Supplementary	
Agriculture	For 1981-82 " 1982-83		
Defence	" 1980 " 1981	1982-83 Winter (no report)	
Education			1980-81 (no report) 1982-83 (no report)
Employment			Manpower Services Commission's Corporate Plan examined 1979-80; 1980-81; 1981-82; 1983-84
Energy	For 1982-82	1983-84 1983-84 Summer	
Environment	For 1984-83 " 1984-85 Property Services Agency	1982-83 Winter	1980-81 (Housing) 1981-82 (Housing)

Table 2 continued

Foreign Affairs	1980-81 (no report) 1981-82 1982-83 1983-84 (no report)	1982-83 (Winter, no report)	1982-83 (Spring)
Home Affairs		None	
Industry & Trade Scottish Affairs		None	1980-81 (no report) 1981-82 (no report) 1982-83 (no report) 1983-84 (no report)
Social Services			1980-81 1981-82 1982-83 1983-84
Transport			1980-81 1981-82 1982-83 1983-84
Treasury & Civil Services	1980-81 1984-85	1970-80 Spring 1981-82 Spring 1981-82 Summer 1982-83 Spring	

Table 2 continued

Welsh Affairs   1980-81   1980-81

by the Environment Committee, the Road Programme by the Transport Committee received regular consideration. However, in the early years of their operation the committees were 'constrained from doing more' in the examination of expenditure for two reasons, as the Liaison Committee report explained. [6] There was the need for extra staff to assist the committees to carry out the necessary detailed examination and there was also a need to ensure that opportunities were provided in the House to debate the reports resulting from such inquiries. Without such opportunities, the committees were reluctant to devote existing resources to expenditure inquiries.

The widely held belief that everything Governments do have financial implications and therefore all inquiries into Government activities concern public expenditure did not invalidate the need for expenditure scrutiny by Parliament in detail and independently from the consideration of wider issues.

The opportunities for Parliament to do so have been regarded as unsatisfactory by most. In one of their first reports the chairman of the Treasury & Civil Service Committee called the "present system a farce" [7] and recommended the examination of Supply procedures by the Procedure Committee. The resulting Procedure Committee inquiry concluded with the recommendation to provide guaranteed debating time for the Estimates to replace the Supply Days, which had long ceased to be concerned with Supply. In response to the recommendation from the Procedure Committee 3 new Estimate Days were created [8] in 1982, as against the 8 days recommended by the Procedure Committee. The Estimate Days are reserved for the consideration of Estimates selected by the Liaison Committee, preferably, but not necessarily, on the basis of reports from the departmental select committees.

There is not much evidence to date that the increased and guaranteed debating opportunities led to an upsurge of interest in the examination of Estimates by the committees. Between 1979 and 1984 the committees spent only 5 per cent of their time in the consideration of Estimates and there were no noticeable changes after 1982.

Some important questions were raised in the course of such inquiries about the accuracy of particular Estimates (Social Service, Defence Treasury) about the inadequacy of the information provided (Employment, Treasury, Energy) and about the need for regular up-to-date information on annual changes (Agriculture).

Most committees made it abundantly clear that they wished to be better informed; there was ample criticism of individual departments for lack of co-operation, and few escaped from it. At the same time, many a critical word was passed about the Treasury playing the part of the "Scrooge of Whitehall". Anxious inquiries about the adequacy of public expenditure provisions (Transport) or congratulations on getting more money out of the Treasury (Education & Arts) were not unheard. Neither were committees adverse to putting forward recommendations for increased expenditure on various projects; for instance, for increased YTS allowance, for increased long-term supplementary benefits for the over 50s, for funding for the development of the PWR, and others.

Though the committees managed to combine their genuine desire for more and better information about expenditure with taking in turn to be champions of their departments or judiciously critical of their handling of public funds, their interest in expenditure was clearly not central to their work. Nor did interest increase noticeably when there were significant changes in the share of particular departments within the allocation of public expenditure.

Committees which annually considered expenditure plans included Foreign Affairs, whose share of PE declined from 2.8% in 78-79 to 1.9% in 82-83; Social Service, whose share of PE increased from 36.4% in 78-79 to 40.1% in 82-83; and Transport, whose share of PE practically unchanged, 3.7% in 78-79 and 3.8% in 82-83.

Committees usually paid some attention to those specific projects or programmes within a department's budget which showed significant changes and not only when expenditure was increasing. The Finances of BSC with its increasing support from the Industry & Trade budget (from 0.6% in 78-79 to 4.8% in 1982-83) received annual attention from the Industry & Trade Committee, as did British Rail from the Transport Committee, Housing received annual attention from the Environment Committee, although housing expenditure declined from 61% of the departmental budget in 78-79 to 43% in 1982-83.

Support for the coal industry, with its increasing claim on the Energy Budget (49% in 1978-79, 71% in 82-83), received less consistent attention from the Energy Committee during the early years. The Committee felt constrained by the lack of a formal role in the consideration of the Estimates, "... if we had such formal role, we would have been extremely reluctant to endorse extra expenditure for the coal industry" said their report in

1982. [9] The more regular interest recently shown by the Committee in the support of the coal industry, however owes as much to the political significance of the 1984 coal strike as to the introduction of the Estimate Days and the opportunities they created for debating committee reports.

Only in the case of the Treasury & Civil Service Committee can it be said with some justification that the examination of public expenditure plans had a central place in their annual programme of inquiries. As the committee responsible for monitoring all aspects of the work of the Treasury, they considered it incumbent on themselves to examine the Government's Expenditure Plans each year as presented in the annual White Paper, and to produce their report on it in time for the debate on the White Paper. However, even in the case of the Treasury & Civil Service Committee these inquiries accounted for only a small fraction of the work carried out each session. The majority of their inquiries, as of all other committees, concerned other major issues which it would not be accurate to describe as the monitoring of departmental expenditure.

NOTES

[1]   Flegmann, V. Focus on Policy Issues in the Work of the Departmental Select Committees of the House of Commons. Paper to the European Consortium for Political Research. Freiburg, March 1983, p. 15.

[2]   Ibid p. 5.

[3]   Robinson, A. op cit. p. 103.

[4]   see (2).

[5]   1st Report from the Liaison Committee, 1982-83. HC.92.

[6]   Ibid p. 11.

[7]   1 Special Report, Treasury & Civil Service Committee 1979-80 HC.503, p.v.

[8]   New Standing Order 19. (Erskine May, 20th Edition).

[9]   2 Report from the Energy Committee 1981-82.   HC.231 p.xviii.

4 The role of select committees in the control of public expenditure — Members' views

Though the role of committees is defined at the time of their appointment, the work they will actually do reflects the way in which members themselves see their duties. No Standing Order has ever been so precisely drawn as to defeat the intention of members to place their own interpretation on their duties. Even in the case of the PAC, the doyen of select committees and with the most precisely drawn terms of reference, such interpretation is possible. For the new select committees appointed in 1979 the Order of Reference was deliberately drawn to allow different interpretations.

The programme committees carry out is determined by a combination of long-term considerations, unavoidable topical urgencies, the need to make an impact, and the need to be seen to have made an impact. It frequently also bears the imprints of the views of strong personalities. Not much of this becomes apparent from reading the published records of committee proceedings. Even when committees divide during the consideration of their report there are few indications of the strengths of conflicting views and of the lengths of discussions which preceded the agreed final reports. A careful scrutiny of verbatim records of evidence sessions is more revealing and watching committees at work is both informative and fascinating. Debates in the House provide useful opportunities for Members to publicise their views, but are

unlikely to be used to air views dissenting from the agreed
report.

Increasingly, Members make statements to the press and media
on reports or on inquiries in progress; articles by Members in
journals and newspapers are additional sources of information
on their attitudes.

Valuable as all these opportunities are, they have one
serious shortcoming in common: most of them reveal what Members
consider important but allow little chance to discover why they
choose to concentrate on certain issues in preference to
others, and none at all to discuss their reasons for doing so.

A somewhat more useful opportunity was provided by the 1982
conference organised by the Industry and Parliament Trust [1]
on the new select committee system where "practitioners of ...
the new aspects of British Parliament" met to assess the
working of the new system. The conference provided an
opportunity for discussion, but mainly on the basis of papers
presented, all of which were aiming to provide general
assessments rather than discussions of specific questions.
Only during personal interviews with committee Members can such
questions be raised.

In 1984 a series of interviews was carried out by the author
with long-standing [2] and active [3] committee Members from
the major parties. The purpose of the interviews was twofold:
First, to find out how Members saw the role of select
committees in the monitoring of departmental expenditure, and
what were the factors which shaped their views; further, to
discover what committee Members regarded as the major
achievements of the committees in their first 5 years and how
they saw the future developments of their tasks.

1. EXPENDITURE

The most commonly held view was that the examination of
departmental expenditure should be carried out as part of the
examination of Government policies, and only occasionally was
there a need to consider specific projects or programmes. Less
than 20% of those interviewed regarded the annual examination
of public expenditure plans for individual departments as
useful, and nearly two years after the establishment of
Estimate Days, only 10 per cent saw it as their duty to examine
the Main or Supplementary Estimates.

This was in contrast with the avowed enthusiasm for the

introduction of the Estimate Days, which most regarded as a significant new development, though they were not quite sure how to make the best use of them. There were a few voices which recalled the fate of the old Supply Days and saw some danger of the Estimate Days developing in the same direction and becoming occasions for general political debate.

Not only was there no enthusiasm for the consideration of figures in detail, but there was surprisingly little for asking more general questions about departmental expenditure with respect to value for money (VFM). Lack of resources to carry out such work was seen as a major obstacle by about half of the Members who declared themselves to be interested in undertaking VFM inquiries, closely followed by their scepticism about the willingness of fellow committee members to become involved in such work. The other half of those interviewed regarded VFM to be within the ambit of the PAC and not of the departmental committees.

Lack of interest and indeed awareness was specially marked about the purpose, operation and progress of the Financial Management Initiative Programme (FMI) [4] launched in May 1982 to improve the allocation, management and control of resources throughout central government. Only about 10 per cent of those interviewed had some idea of the Programme, though even they did not expect to make much use of the information resulting from it.

The discovery giving the greatest ground for concern however, was the frank admission from 20 per cent of active, long established committee members that they had little interest in public expenditure. Even those who did not admit to such disinterest, showed little inclination to devote more of their time to the consideration of finance. Although several Members mentioned the possibility of setting up financial sub-committees, as an answer to the problem, only one followed up this suggestion by indicating his willingness to participate in such. Others, who thought these would be useful, quickly added, "... but not for me". There were a variety of reasons given.
The first and main one on everyone's list was the question of resources and this generally implied the shortage of their own time. MPs are more realistic than is usually assumed about how much use they can make of additional assistance and they have a strong and justified aversion to the ever increasing mound of papers landing on their desks. More research assistants would certainly be needed if they were to embark on more detailed financial scrutiny but "more assistants churned out more papers but not the time for reading them" was heard repeatedly.

MPs also believed that the work they do on committees goes largely unnoticed and unappreciated, even when they are examining some of the topical issues of the day. If they were to devote more of their time to the consideration of finance, their constituents would know even less about what they were doing in Westminster.

To a considerable extent MPs see the consideration of public expenditure in terms of 'spending more' or 'spending less' rather than spending well, as their earlier discussed lack of interest in VFM demonstrated. A surprising number of them therefore regarded the consideration of expenditure to be 'too politically sensitive' for a bipartisan examination by select committees.

2. ACHIEVEMENTS

Given the muted enthusiasm for getting involved in the examination of finances, Members, predictably, did not rate their achievements in improving the parliamentary scrutiny of public expenditure very high. It must be added however, that in general, they did not have an over-inflated view of the impact of their work.

A number of particular inquiries were cited as having had a decisive influence on Government actions. These were the Home Affairs Committee report on the 'sus-law', the Foreign Affairs Committee report on the British North America Act, the Energy Committee report on Nuclear Power, the Social Services Committee report on Sick Pay and others, but only one, the Treasury and Civil Service Committee report in 1981-82, [5] for its contribution to improved expenditure control. It was on the basis of the recommendations of this report, that regular Annual Autumn Statements were introduced on the Government expenditure plans with revenue, expenditure and borrowing projections.

Members, without exception, regarded the improved flow of information to Parliament and to the public as the most significant achievement of the new committees.

There is a widely held belief among committee members that Debates are better informed as a consequence of committee inquiries especially since the introduction of the practice of 'tags' (italicized reference) on the Order Papers indicating committee reports relevant to the debates of the day.

Considerable importance is attached to the role of committees in bringing to the notice of Parliament a wide range of views about the issues under consideration, but this is seldom relevant in connection with 'finance inquiries' where the witnesses are usually Ministers or civil servants.

Committee Members also believe that the impact of their work is only partially reflected in the number of reports debated, recommendations accepted and acted on or in the various identifiable measures introduced as a consequence of their activities.

They believe that Governments now frequently wait for committees to express their views before final decisions are made, and Whitehall decision-making now includes, as a matter of course, some assessment of likely committee reactions. This belief was, in fact, endorsed by Lord Diamond, the former Chief Secretary to the Treasury in his book [6] when he wrote "... Committee questioning and criticism often succeed in such variations in the future implementation of the programme or such modification in policy as would achieve more efficiency and greater value for money."

It was to safeguard both this 'general impact', as well as the chance to influence specific decisions, that Members placed the greatest emphasis on the need for unanimous reports. All regarded this as extremely important, and more than half considered it essential; all recognised that the price of unanimity is some measure of compromise.

Some regarded the need to make the necessary compromises to be met by the choice of subjects for inquiries: 'we must be realistic', 'we need to take a pragmatic approach'. Others expected the 'uncontestable facts' to bring about the needed unanimity; on those, 'men of good will' tend to agree. Even if long and bitter arguments precede the consideration of the draft report, Members usually recognise that the impact of a unanimous report is significantly greater than that of a divided one, and finally do agree on the report. One Member, himself not adverse to taking very definite minority views, added that even a minority report would usually necessitate some compromise and thus was not worth it.

Members saw little need for and little likelihood of any major changes in the future in the nature, range or scope of committee work, and certainly none which would significantly increase their role in relation to departmental expenditure. They believed there will be a considerable competition for time on Estimate Days and at most expected to have an occasional report of their own on some Supplementary Estimates to be debated. They did not think that this would make necessary any changes in their approach to their tasks and expected to continue spending most of their time in the consideration of Government policy. Some thought it likely that select committees might become involved in pre-legislative scrutiny in an attempt to improve the quality of legislation. Others from committees with no power to appoint sub-committees were hoping to have this granted; and all hoped for freer flow of information from Government and the departments, and for speedier responses to their recommendations.

Members appear to be able to accommodate a surprising number of self conflicting views about committee work, Government, Whitehall and a variety of other issues without apparent difficulty.
They complain about the flood of papers reaching them, yet ask for more. They complain about the lack of recognition given to their work by Parliament, yet consider their most important achievement the improved Debates following their reports. They frequently make the distinction between co-operation received from Government and a department, only to criticise both for obstructing committee inquiries. Most amazing of all, they regard themselves as being both bipartisan and highly political at the same time in their committee work.

The views of Whitehall were found to be somewhat different.

NOTES

[1]   Commons Select Committees: Catalysts for Progress?
      Ed. Dermot Englefield, Longman 1984.
[2]   'Long-standing' was interpreted as continuous
      membership since 1979.
[3]   Activity was assessed on the basis of high attendance
      and participation at committee meetings.
[4]   Efficiency and Effectiveness in the Civil Service.
      Cmnd. 8616.
[5]   6R Treasury & Civil Service Committee 1981-82.
      HC.137. Budgetary Reform
[6]   Lord Diamond, Public Expenditure in Practice George
      Allen & Unwin, 1975, p. 113.

5 The role of select committees in the control of public expenditure — Departmental views

There was considerable interest in Whitehall in the early months of 1979 in the proposed select committee reform. Views were fairly uniform on the likely consequences of the establishment of a new, extensive select committee system on the work of the departments.

During a series of interviews conducted in the Spring of 1979, [1] all but one of the 14 Permanent Secretaries asked thought the principle of such a system unexceptionable, though half of them had some doubts about the operation of the system in practice. Some of the doubts concerned the extra workload which would have to be carried by the departments in consequence of increased committee activities; others concerned the ability of such committees to carry out their investigations in a sufficiently bipartisan manner. Senior civil servants regarded bipartisanship to be an essential ingredient for any inquiry if it was to lead to a useful report, whatever its subject.

Although there was general agreement that much of the new committees' attention would be taken up by questioning Ministers on Government policies, '... they will try to give Ministers a tough time', Whitehall expected the committees to take considerable interest in their own work, especially in the way they manage public expenditure programmes. 'In view of the amount of public funds we dispose of, this would be right and proper'. In general, Whitehall were confident in their ability to cope with any demands made on them by a new system, even if not actually enthusiastic to undertake the additional workload involved in supplying committees with papers. They also expected to benefit, however, from the extra attention they would receive in the form of better understanding in Westminster of the workings of the departments, and of some of the difficulties of implementing Government decisions.

In 1984, a new round of interviews were carried out in Whitehall to establish the impact of the new select committee system on the work of the departments, to discover whether the more extended committee activities made any positive contribution to financial management and what, in the view of senior civil servants, were the likely and desirable future developments.

Yet again, as in 1979, the views expressed by the twenty senior civil servants most involved with the work of the committees (giving evidence, briefing Ministers) were very much in agreement. They confirmed that Whitehall expectations at the inception of the new committee system were remarkably accurate in many, though not all, aspects.

The increased committee activities in Westminster undoubtedly led to greater demands for information from the departments on a wider and wider range of subjects, though not significantly on expenditure plans or Estimates. On average, about 300 departmental memoranda are submitted to the committees each session; seldom more than 5 per cent of them are concerned with the examination of expenditure.

Whitehall accepted the increased direct parliamentary demand on them with commendable equanimity. Indeed most of them thought it actually useful for the departments to prepare and present information for inquires and committees hardly ever call for data which have to be specially collected for the purpose. Even on such occasions the information collected might become useful subsequently. They had some doubts, however, about how much use committee members make of the data provided by the departments at the committees' request and would clearly appreciate an early indication of specific interests so they could provide more of the relevant and less of the unnecessary information. Civil servants are mindful of MPs' problems in the face of an ever-mounting volume of documents, and would prefer to provide what committee members could actually use.

There were far fewer complaints about the extra work for

departments than the frequency of Parliamentary Questions about it would suggest. The number of civil service man-hours spent on committee work appears to exercise the minds of MPs more than civil servants. When some approximate calculations are made on the basis of replies to such questions, the reason becomes apparent; the burden in fact is not excessive. As an example, in the 1980-81 session, civil service time on committee-related activities in the case of the Foreign Affairs Committee was estimated to be "1325 man-days" [2]. On the basis of the grade of civil servants involved, at the salary level in operation at the time, the cost of this was calculated to have been about £63,000 out of the total civil service cost of some £76 m on the FO Vote. [3] This was the Committee which had had the largest number of meetings, received the largest number of civil service memoranda in that year and whose witnesses were mostly Ministers and civil servants.

Civil service expectations about being able to cope with increased committee demands were thus confirmed. Their prediction for the committees' proclivity to haul an increasing number of Ministers in front of them had also been amply confirmed. In the first year alone, there were 40 Ministerial appearances in front of the committees, and the tendency did not abate, as figures on p. 20 demonstrated.

The burden of giving oral evidence to select committees has shifted dramatically from civil servants to Ministers since 1979. The Expenditure Committee took evidence from Ministers and civil servants at a ratio of 1 Minister to 40 civil servants; for the departmental committees the ratio now is 1 Minister to 4 civil servants. The consequence of this change is not necessarily a corresponding reduction in the work of civil servants but certainly a change in the nature of the work involved and might explain departmental attitudes to the new committees to some extent. Since committee inquiries make it necessary for Ministers to be briefed in detail about an increasing range of their departments' activities, such briefings provide additional opportunities to convey departmental views to Ministers. Without suggesting that these opportunities are in any sense 'exploited for some devious departmental purposes', they are certainly used fully.

Not all of the senior civil servants' expectations were, however, fulfilled and the new committees did both surprise and disappoint Whitehall.

The committees proved to be impressively bipartisan in the manner they carried out their investigations and largely managed to avoid the pitfalls of becoming either too cosy or too hostile in their attitude to 'their' department. Much of the credit for this is attributed to the chairmen who made every effort to curb any persistent attempts at politicising committee meetings. For 'a bunch of professional politicians', committee members were considered remarkably bipartisan.

Members in general also impressed Whitehall with their capacity for hard work and their ability to become 'competent amateurs'.

Disappointment was largely the result of the lack of interest committees showed in departmental expenditure, and in particular in the way the departments introduced changes to improve the management and implementation of public expenditure programmes. The lack of interest by the committees in the introduction of the Financial Management Initiative Programme and in the progress made since 1982 by individual departments came as a considerable surprise and in most cases also as some disappointment. Given the new committees' order of reference which included the examination of expenditure, policy and administration, they fully expected the committees to take advantage of the additional information about the working of the departments which FMI provides. Civil servants recognised that a sudden, widespread interest would create problems for them, but nonetheless expect Parliament to take a greater interest in their measures to improve efficiency than hitherto expressed. The programme was, after all, launched in consequence of the inquiry carried out by the new Treasury and Civil Service Committee, so not unreasonably they expected more continued interest in its development.

Inevitably, there were some critical comments on a confidential, non-attributable basis about past inquiries, about committees 'missing the point', 'opening the cupboard but not noticing the skeleton' or occasionally 'going off at a tangent'. In most cases, senior civil servants could think of subjects which, in their view, would have merited committee attention but did not receive it. Equally, they could and did name inquiries which, in their views, were the most important ones, only a few of which were directly concerned with the planning or management of public expenditure. Among these the Treasury and Civil Service Committee report leading to the introduction of the regular Annual Autumn Statement clearly ranked as the most important, closely followed by the inquiry which led to the introduction of the FMI, and civil servants seem to have attached noticeably more importance to the examination of Estimates than MPs did.

Civil servants also seemed to be fully aware of the impact

of strong personalities on the work of individual committees, and not necessarily always that of the chairman. Committee interests and style of working were frequently associated with individual members by name. This was in noticeable contrast with references made by MPs, who invariably referred to 'civil servants' and often even to 'Ministers' in preference to named individuals.

For the future, the departments clearly expect the committees to show a greater interest in the Estimates as a consequence of the introduction of the new Estimate Days, and to take a closer and harder look at expenditure proposals, to which the Treasury indicated [4] they had no objection.

Civil servants saw some danger of over=proliferation of committee inquiries which could reduce the quality of the reports and thus their impact. This would also endanger the regular follow=up of progress made on implementing earlier recommendations which all regarded as very important. Some already thought follow=up was inadequate. It was partly on this count that about half of the senior civil servants interviewed thought that select committees should not have a formal role in pre=legislative scrutiny. Although all made a point of emphasizing the 'special' character and problems of their department, and as a consequence thought their comments might well be very different from the comments of their colleagues in other parts of Whitehall, there was in fact a remarkable consensus of views scattered around the departments, as indeed there was in Westminster. As Lord Hailsham put it, though in a somewhat different context, [5] "any honest man, given the same information is bound to come to the same conclusions..."

Whitehall's assessment of the new select committees, and of the impact of their inquiries on the management of public funds, may well not have been any more or any less accurate than were MPs' own evaluations of their own achievements. There is a need to consider a variety of indicators which can be regarded as measures of the committees' achievements, which make up the composite and complex picture of what has been accomplished in the first 5 years.

NOTES

[1]   Flegmann, V. Government Departments and Select Committees of the House of Commons, Paper presented at the Political Studies Association, Annual Conference, Hull, 1981.

[2] Reply to PQ, Hansard Vol. 22/23, cl. 246-7.
[3] Flegmann, V. Focus on Policy Issues, op. cit. p. 8.
[4] 6R T & CS Cttee 1981-82. HC. 137. Q.151.
[5] Lord Hailsham, op. cit. p. 159.

PART III

6 The achievements of the early years

There are as yet no fully satisfactory measures for the assessment of the achievements of past or present select committees, nor are there likely to be any in the future. A range of indicators has to be considered, but the relative weight attached to each must by necessity be subjective.

The contribution of the departmental committees in providing additional information for the scrutiny of Government policies is indisputable. There are few issues of current or future policy which did not benefit from committee attention and the volume of comments and recommendations together with an impressively wide range of 'expert views' on subjects ranging from Animal Welfare to Strategic Nuclear Weapons or the Age of Retirement are awaiting the interested MPs in the House of Commons Library.

Similarly, much additional information on public expenditure became available to the House as a consequence of committee activities.

Some of the major achievements in this area are well known and well publicised. No one would dispute that the most important among them was the introduction of the regular annual Autumn Statement following the inquiry and recommendations from the Treasury and Civil Service Committee referred to earlier.

Also, largely from the Treasury & Civil Service Committee, came the other most important recommendations for improved financial information and increased parliamentary opportunities for their consideration.

The inquiry into the Supplementary Estimates in 1980 [1] set in motion the wheels which, after inquiry and report from the Procedure Committee, [2] came to rest with the establishment of the Estimate Days in 1982.

The initial impetus for the launching of the FMI, very much a central issue in Whitehall, even if as yet not in Westminster, also came from a report from the Treasury & Civil Service Committee. [3] The data becoming available from this programme could well prove to be the most significant source of information for select committees, and thus for Parliament, on how public expenditure decisions are implemented.

Additional and improved information in the PE White Paper became available about a variety of programmes and projects as a result of pressures from a number of departmental select committees. Some examples are the effects of the Common Agricultural Policy (CAP) price-fixing on the Estimates (Agriculture), additional explanatory notes to the Defence Statement (Defence), information on various Government initiatives to provide low-cost housing (Environment), disaggregated figures for PE in Scotland (Scottish Affairs), and the reserve list for road construction schemes (Transport). The lion's share in pressing for such information again has been that of the Treasury & Civil Service Committee with their repeated calls for more comprehensive White Papers with introductory notes on each Vote, more narrative information and other similar requests.

The opportunities for the House to take advantage of the greater availability of financial information, also increased, if somewhat more modestly.

Until the advent of the Estimate Days, no committee reports on the Estimates on PE were a subject for debate, though ten reports were 'noted as relevant to the debate of the day on the Order Paper', (8 from the Treasury & Civil Service, and 2 from the Defence Committee) by the summer of 1983.

The introduction of the Estimate Days both increased the debating opportunities and extended it to reports from a wider range of committees. Table 3 shows how Estimate Days were allocated during the first two years after their introduction.

Table 3. Use of Estimate Days, March 1983 to March 1985

Date	Reports Debated	Subject
14.3.1983	2R T & CS Cttee 82-83 2R Foreign Aff. 82-83	HMSO Vote Supplem. Est. Turk's & Caicos Islands (Dev.) Suppl. Est.
8.3.84	Public Accounts Cttee 2R Energy Cttee 83-84	Compensation Payment for NHS staff Grants to NCB (Compensation to redundant workers)
4.7.84	2R Education Cttee 82-83 2R Environment 83-84 Public Accounts Cttee	Prison Education D. of Environment Estimates Dog Licences
17.7.84	2 & 4R Foreign Affairs 3R Environment 83-84 Public Accounts Cttee	FCO & ODC Estimates; & Grenada Property Services Agency Estimates (Maintenance)
18.12.84	4R Energy 83-84 5R Foreign Affairs	BNOC Winter Supplementary Est.
14.3.85	5R Energy Cttee 84-85	Industrial Support

The majority of MPs taking part in the debates however, were committee members already familiar with the content of the reports and the issues raised, and there is little evidence so far of an increasing interest in these debates among non-committee members.

It would almost be true to say that increased parliamentary awareness of the work of the committee owes as much to the publicity which their reports, and from time to time their evidence sessions, receive from the media, as to the additional debating opportunities provided by the Estimate Days. Regular press conferences on the publication of reports and an extensive provision of press notices about current and forthcoming inquiries ensures that the 'quality' papers are able to provide prompt coverage of the 'newsworthy' items. Many backbenchers admit to getting their first intimation of committee inquiries or the substance of their reports through the media.

Regrettably, the inquiries which concentrate on the financial scrutiny role are seldom considered 'newsworthy' and a considerable body of information revealed in the course of the inquiries goes unreported and largely un-noticed. Some examples are worth mentioning.

For instance, the inquiry into the 1984 Defence Estimates [4] revealed that a one cent move in the rate of exchange against the dollar means a £25 m change in the cost of Trident (original prices in 1980 were based on £1 = $2.36).

The inquiry into the Scottish aspects of the 1982-85 PE White Paper [5] 'discovered' the Barnett Formula, applied since 1978 for allocating PE changes between England, Scotland and Wales (England 85%, Scotland 19%, Wales 5%).

The discussion which took place during the consideration of the FCO Estimates 1982-83 [6] about the Government's decision to increase fees for overseas students, revealed much concern about the 'malign consequences' of this decision for future Anglo-Chinese relations for example.

Discussing future social security spending in 1980 [7] the Social Services Committee warned that "...the Contingency Fund may be largely pre-empted if the ... assumptions about unemployment turn out to be unrealistic". (They did turn out to be unrealistic, the estimated 1.8 m for 1981-82 in Cmnd. 7841, in reality became 2.8 m in 1982 [8] and substantial increases in the Contingency Reserve followed for 1982-83 and subsequent years).

Even conclusions such as that by the inquiry of the Environment Committee into the Financing of Local Government that "... the abolition of the domestic rating system would not command widespread support and would not be justified" [9] did not receive the attention it merited.

Although the reports of the committees following their examination of Estimates or other expenditure projections did not often make the headlines, nor proved to be material for Debates which filled the benches of the House, they have made a significant impact in Whitehall in a variety of forms.

Some reports draw attention to departmental errors such as those in the Estimates for Maintenance Expenditure in the case of the Property Services Agency (debated on Estimate Day 17.7.1984); to the lack of provision in the Department of Environment Main Estimates for the London Zoo, which necessitated Supplementary Estimates for successive years [10] or to a missing footnote, spotted in the Supplementary Estimates for the Welsh Office, [11] customary in cases where the authority for the proposed expenditure is the Estimate itself. Measures to correct them followed. A variety of recommendations led to specific measures ranging from the introduction of oral language examinations for diplomatic staff above a certain grade [12] to providing the final impetus for long overdue major measures such as the re-organisation of the Ministry of Defence. [13]

From time to time, committee reports and recommendations strengthened the hand of the departments in their negotiations with the Treasury as in the case of end-of-year carry-over provisions on the Defence [14] and the Transport Vote. [15]

Select committee inquiries into major projects or major programmes, of course, did include some detailed financial considerations and such inquiries occupied a significant part of the committees' timetable. The most important ones are presented in Table 4.

The list is by no means exhaustive, as committee Members repeatedly pointed out. Anything Government does has serious financial implications, and no inquiry can be concerned purely with policy. Nonetheless, while committees did comment on financial issues during the course of a wide range of inquiries or did make recommendations which led to improved monitoring by the House or to better financial management by the departments, none would claim to have had this as their primary aim.

Over and above the specific, identifiably impact of select

Table 4. Select Committee Inquiries Concerning Major
Projects and Programmes

Committee	Subject of Inquiry	Session
Agriculture	Organisation & Financing of Agricultural R & D	1982-83; 1983-84
Defence	Sting Ray	1980-81
	Strategic Nuclear Weapons	1980-81; 1981-82
	MOD Organisation & Procurement	1981-82
Education & Arts	Funding & Organisation of courses in Higher Education	1979-80
	Public & Private Funding of Arts	1980-81
Employment	Manpower Services Commission Corporate Plan	annually
Energy	Industrial Energy Pricing	1980-81
	Electricity & Gas Prices	1983-84
Environment	Housing	some aspects of it in each session
Foreign Affairs	Overseas Student Fees: aid implications	1979-80
	The work of the Commonwealth Development Corporation	1981-82
Home Affairs	British Nationality Fees	1982-83
Industry & Trade	The Post Office	1979-80: 1981-82
	British Steel Corporation	annually
	British Leyland	80-81;81-82; 83-84
	Concorde	80-81;81-82
	Rolls Royce	1981-82
Scottish Affairs	Housing Capital Allocation	1980-81
	Steel Industry in Scotland	1982-83

48

Table 4. continued

Committee	Subject of Inquiry	Session
Social Services	Sick pay proposals	1980-81
	The Griffith Report on NHS Management	1983-84
Transport	The road programme	80-81;81-82; 82-83
	Main line electrification	1981-82
	The Serpell Report on Railway Finances	1981-82
	Organisation, Financing & Control of Airports	1983-84
Treasury & CS	Civil Service Manpower	79-80;80-81; 81-82;82-83
Welsh Affairs	Water in Wales	1982-83
	Impact of Regional Industrial Policy in Wales	1 9 8 3 - 8 4

committee inquiries, the continued, even if peripheral, interest of the committees in departmental expenditure is also having a noticeable influence on attitudes in Whitehall.

The recognition that major policy decisions in most cases must anticipate some rigorous scrutiny from the relevant select committee established then in the eyes of civil servants as a force which must be taken into consideration in all aspects of their work. The examination of Estimates might at present not be regular, and might even be cursory when it happened but few in the civil service believed this was likely to remain so. Already the effort which goes into preparation for examination by the committees on departmental expenditure is far in excess of what in practice turns out to have been necessary, but no civil servant would care to take the risk of appearing unprepared for examination by a select committee. There is a feeling in Whitehall that such examinations could at any time turn more searching, more detailed, perhaps more hostile, but also perhaps more useful. For Whitehall watchers some of the most telling signs of the changing climate are the virtual disappearance of comments frequently heard about the Expenditure Committee that civil servants were "educating MPs" during the evidence sessions, and that comparisons between the departmental select committees and the Public Accounts Committee are made less and less frequently.

There is a widely held view, both inside and outside Westminster, that the greatest impact of the new committee system has been on the quality of Government decision making, and the best known instances of direct committee influence are well publicised and documented (the repeal of th 'sus law', the influence on the British North America Act, the change in the statutory sick pay). Others are less well known, such as the role of the Transport Committee in initiating the Serpell Inquiry, the scaling down of the nuclear energy programme following the Energy Committee's inquiry on the subject, and the changing support for the Concorde following the Industry & Trade Committee's inquiries.

Views are divided about the value of calling on Ministers to give evidence in the course of committee inquiries. There is one school of thought which claims that Ministers are happy or even keen to appear in front of the select committees. A different view, held equally firmly, is that few Ministers actually enjoy such occasions and even fewer are those who do not need to spend some considerable time preparing for them (extra briefing etc.). Since Ministers are seldom short of opportunities to put across their views either inside or outside Parliament, there is no reason why they should be eager to do so in front of select committees, where they are invariably subjected to some hostile and persistent questioning, even from some of their own supporters. Nor are Ministers necessarily able to leave committee meetings with the satisfaction of having left behind a committee convinced or converted. However, since the committees appear to be determined to inquire into ever widening areas of Government activities, Ministers in most cases subject themselves to committee examination with tolerably good grace.

One further aspect of the impact of the new select committees need to be considered, and that is the impact on backbenchers themselves who take part in committee work.

Over the past five years, more than 300 MPs have served at one time or other, most of them for some years, on one of the departmental select committees, and 1 in 5 of those appointed after the 1983 Election were committee members since the inception of the new system in 1979. (The largest single cause for membership changes was Members losing their seats or retiring, the second was appointment to office which, though usually junior, nonetheless disqualifies MPs from committe membership). For the majority of backbench MPs, membership on a scrutinizing committee has become an integral part of their parliamentary career and for some a long-term one. This has two important consequences.

First, as a result of their work on committees a growing number of backbenchers are becoming 'expert', in some measure, about particular areas of Government activities. They hear and discuss, sometimes even read, evidence provided by the experts about a variety of topics and then, armed with the knowledge gained, have the opportunity to question those in charge of either formulating or implementing policies.

From this, the second important consequence follows, and that is the increased confidence of backbenchers to question and challenge leaders of their own party and their decisions, both in Government and in Opposition. Perhaps one of the most remarkable facts about the work of the departmental committees is that reports critical of Government policy or action are just as likely to come from committees under a chairmanship from the Government side as from the Opposition, if not more so.

The change in the balance of power between the Executive and the Legislature hoped for and foreseen in 1979 did not happen in exactly the form it was expected. The realignment of forces which did take place was some shift of power from the Front

Benches to Backbenchers, with Backbenchers from all parties presenting a unified front more and more frequently.

Though the committees have tackled an impressive variety of subjects, in some respects they did not fulfil expectations.

NOTES

[1] 1st Special Report, Treasury & Civil Service Committee 1979-80. HC. 503.
[2] 1st Report Select Committee on Procedure (Supply) 1980-81. HC.535.
[3] 3R Treasury & Civil Service Committee 1981-82 HC. 24. Efficiency and Effectiveness in the Civil Service
[4] 1R Defence Committee 1983-84. HC. 436.
[5] Report from the Committee on Scottish Affairs 1981-82. HC. 413.
[6] 3R Foreign Affairs Committee 1981-82. HC. 406.
[7] 3R Social Service Committee 1979-80. HC. 702.
[8] OECD Economic Survey, United Kingdom 1985. P. 39.
[9] 2R, Environment Committee 1981-82. HC. 217.
[10] 2R, Environment Committee 1982-83. HC. 170.
[11] 1R, Welsh Affairs Committee 1980-81. HC. 61.
[12] 4R, Foreign Affairs Committee 1980-81. HC. 343.
[13] 2R, Defence Committee, 1981-82. HC. 22.
[14] 2R, Defence Committee, 1979-80. HC. 302.
[15] 4R, Transport Committee 1981-82. HC. 334.

7 The stones which remained unturned

At the time the departmental select committees were first appointed in 1979 some of the questions about their future role were left unresolved. The two major ones were the formal role of the new committees in the consideration of public expenditure, and the role of the committees in monitoring the nationalised industries. Up to 1979 the latter function was fulfilled by the Select Committee on Nationalised Industries. The new committees were to develop their own approach to both issues, though in the case of monitoring the nationalised industries, provisions for a joint sub-committee from the Energy, Environment, Industry and Trade, Transport and the Treasury & Civil Service Committees were included in the Standing Order.

The initial ambiguity of the new committees' roles in both respects was largely responsible for the inadequate attention devoted to both these areas during the early years. The lack of a formal role in the consideration of the departmental Estimates encouraged the natural inclination of MPs to concentrate on the 'newsworthy' policy issues in preference to finance, taking advantage of the improved opportunities to do so under the new system. After all their predecessor, the Expenditure Committee was said to be 'frustrated' by their inability to consider Government policies. When somewhat belatedly, opportunities were created for committee reports on the Estimates to be debated in the House on a regular basis with the establishment of the 3 Estimate Days, most committees had already decided on the focus of their attention for the coming years, and frequently even had a reserve list of proposed inquiries. Members were beginning to develop the necessary skills for such inquiries, and these were essentially different from those needed for the scrutiny of finance. As Table 2 demonstrates, no committee showed an increased willingness to devote their time to the consideration of Estimates for the uncertain chance of having one of their reports selected by the Liaison Committee for debate on Estimate Day. [1] Having already decided on their priorities, the uncertain chance of a one and a half hour debate did prove to be insufficient inducement to change them. Committee Members neither possessed nor had the inclination to acquire the necessary skills for the detailed scrutiny of Estimates. Had the committees been given this opportunity from the outset and had they been required to consider the Estimates rather than empowered to do so (as the Expenditure Committee report recommended) [2] it is just possible that they would have developed a greater interest in the regular and more thorough examination of Estimates.

For monitoring longer term public expenditure plans the original vagueness of the Standing Order, described as 'permissive', has remained, and attempts to provide the committees with a clearer role in their consideration have so far largely faltered.

Proposals put forward by the Procedure Committee (Finance) [3] in favour of involving departmental select committees in the authorization of major projects was rejected by the Government on the grounds that this would introduce delays, uncertainty, increased administrative costs, and "... would change significantly the respective roles of the Executive and the House, and especially the select committees." [4] Recommendations to increase the involvement of the Treasury & Civil Service Committee in the consideration of public expenditure plans (approval of EFL for the nationalised industries; examination of expenditure from the Consolidated Fund; monitoring Government borrowing on the basis of monthly outturn figures) were similarly rejected by the Government.

Although the recommendations of the Procedure Committee were directed towards the Government, their report was also critical about the extent of financial scrutiny by the House as a whole, "... out of about 170 days, we spend only 16-17 on purely financial matters... and those mainly on taxation" [5]. About the departmental select committees the Procedure Committee noted that, while the main burden of extra work resulting from their recommendations would fall upon the Treasury & Civil Service Committee, the "... other departmental select committees might have to place greater emphasis than hitherto on the financial aspects of their terms of reference if they are to make full use of the opportunities we have given them." [6]

The committees' widely drawn terms of reference cannot be held responsible for the low priority given to the consideration of 'value for money' in their programme. Such questions have long been regarded as the appropriate concern for the committees of the House and an essential part of the parliamentary control of public expenditure. It has even been suggested by a former Chief Secretary to the Treasury that, due to their objective scrutiny, it was unlikely that "... substantial inefficiencies can exist for long in any area of Government spending." [7]

The widespread feeling among committee Members discussed in Chapter 4, that it would be impractical or even unnecessary to spend their time on VFM questions, together with views from Whitehall (considered in Chapter 5) reveal a serious gap in the parliamentary scrutiny of public expenditure.

Repeated references to VFM examinations carried out by the Committee of Public Accounts (PAC) makes it necessary to consider how far the work of this committee can be regarded as sufficient to satisfy Parliament on the economic, efficient and effective use of public funds.

The PAC carry out their inquiries on the basis of the reports of the Comptroller & Auditor General (C & AG) following his examination of departmental accounts, covering about 60% of all public expenditure. With respect to such expenditure he carries out a VFM audit, since 1983 on a statutory basis. The examination is 'accounts-based' and thus takes place when money has already been spent on projects and programmes, and substantial future sums are already committed. In some cases the possibility of introducing changes by the time the examinations are conducted are very limited indeed. For instance, in Defence, 90% of expenditure for the coming year is fixed and any decision taken in the current year will affect only 40% of expenditure in 7 years time" [8]. The series of reports from the C & AG reveal that some earlier, closer scrutiny of expenditure decisions would have been valuable in preventing the necessity of his eventual, critical reports. The C & AG's reports abound with comments on inadequate appraisal of project proposals, weaknesses in planning and control arrangements leading to delays and cost increases in a wide range of projects and programmes. Clearly all such cases would have benefited from critical examination by select committees much earlier.

The launching of the FMI resulted in a flow of information from the departments about how they were going about planning and organising their work for carrying out the policies of the Government. Thus, for the first time, committees are supplied with information on a continuous basis which could have enabled them to carry out detailed scrutiny of selected projects or programmes. So far the departmental committee have showed no inclination to make use of such information, and have regarded FMI largely as a tool for internal management purposes within the departments, with only marginal interest for Parliament.

This view, widely held, indicates another serious shortcoming in the departmental committees' interpretation of their duties as outlined in their order of reference. While the interest shown by the committees in departmental expenditure is certainly inadequate, patchy and uneven, the interest they have shown so far in departmental administration is hardly visible. Within the FMI information about both expenditure and administration are becoming available and could thus enable the committees to take a more balanced approach to their tasks in the future. Neglecting their opportunities to do so could have farreaching consequences (which will be considered in Chapter 9).

There has been no attempt to co-ordinate the monitoring of the nationalised industries by the different committees shadowing the sponsoring departments, although the need for such co-ordination has been foreseen in 1979. There were no attempts from any of the committees to continue with the annual examination of reports and accounts of individual industries, which was an essential part of the work of the Select Committee on Nationalised Industries and was regarded by many, not least by the industries themselves, as useful. Monitoring of the nationalised industries has become one of the many tasks committees now set themselves or, which they find themselves obliged to undertake. It became the centre of their attention only when made inevitable by some Government decision or outside events such as the proposed increase in gas and electricity prices for 1984-85, or the need for increased support for the coal industry in consequence of the coal strike.

The need for a more co-ordinated approach to the monitoring of the nationalised industries is gradually becoming apparent, in response to the recent Treasury proposals for a new legislative framework for the nationalised industries. The Treasury has co-ordinated the views of the sponsoring departments on the proposal but no similar exercise has been undertaken on behalf of the industries concerned by the select committees. Such proposals would have received much attention from the old Select Committee on Nationalised Industries and a recent seminar on this subject [9] revealed a widely felt need by the industries for a more co-ordinated parliamentary approach to some of their problems.

The provisions for a nationalised industries sub-committee included in SO 99 are clearly inadequate, since they did not "identify the select committee to which the sub-committee should report," [10] and as a consequence such a sub-committee would not be able to report on their findings to the House. This inadequacy in the Standing Order is partly responsible for the lack of any attempt to set up such a sub-committee so far, though there are a variety of subjects which would merit their attention. Some of these are at present claiming the time of the Treasury & Civil Service Committee like EFL, others are not yet receiving regular attention from select committees. The most important among them is the examination of actions taken in response to the recommendations of the Monopolies and Mergers Commission in their reports on efficiency inquiries carried out under the 1980 Competition Act.

There are a number of measures which could be taken to widen the scope of the committees' work in the future and to bring it closer to the original intentions of the 1979 select committee reform.

NOTES

[1]   Estimate Days are reserved for debating Estimates recommended by the Liaison Committee usually, but not necessarily, on the basis of reports from select committees.
[2]   11R Expenditure Committee 1976-77, HC. 535. p.161-6.
[3]   1R Select Committee on Procedure 1982-83. HC. 24
[4]   Hansard, 6 December 1983, cl. 290.
[5]   1R Select Committee on Procedure 1982-83. op. cit. p. 9.
[6]   Ibid., p. xlviii 1981-82
[7]   Lord Diamond, Public Expenditure in Practice op. cit. p. 112.
[8]   2R Defence Committee 1979-80. HC. 571. P. xvi.

[9]   Public Finance Foundation, Seminar 20 February
       1985.
[10]   Erskine May, op. cit. p. 707.

8 Changes for the future

Some of the changes which would be needed to allow the new committee system to operate more effectively could be generated within the committees themselves, others would require authorization by the House.

The time has now come for the House to grant all select committees the right to set up sub-committees from time to time, with powers to continue without need for further authorization for the duration of a Parliament. During the 1977 Procedure Committee's inquiry the Clerk of the House suggested that granting such powers should be reconsidered at a later stage, in the light of experience. [1] Only three of the fourteen committees have been granted powers to appoint sub-committees so far; others can only divide informally and only if this does not involve delegation of authority, e.g. for the drafting of reports.

The advantage of allowing select committees unrestricted rights to form sub-committees are manifold and of greater significance than a simple procedural change would imply at a first glance. Smaller, more specialised, groups of MPs are better able to carry out their role of scrutinizing particular subjects. A committee of 11 Members does not allow much detailed questioning by all within the time available and as a result most evidence taking is either monopolised by a handful of specially interested and well informed Members or takes the form of a great variety of not particularly searching questions. The attendance of members at committee meetings, calculated to have been just under 75% for 1979-83 [2] hides considerable variations in the active participation of the examination of witnesses and also considerable differences in frequencies of attendance at meetings, depending on the subject under consideration. In practice, inquiries which require some detailed knowledge or homework, (those concerning finance certainly come into this category) are frequently attended only by the members who are prepared to do the necessary work. Examination of attendance and participation statistics at committee meetings inquiring into Estimates or Public Expenditure Plans during the 1981-82 session revealed that, though attendance at the meetings was usually lower than average, all those present took an active part in the examination of the witnesses. Thus, committees did in practice form themselves into sub-committees without formal authorization and members who had no interest in the subject under consideration simply stayed away. If the informal trend received official recognition it would allow parallel inquiries to be carried out by members with interests in different aspects of their committee's remit.

The House should revoke the provisions for a joint nationalised industries sub-committee since this is unused and unusable, and reconsider the case for a new select committee for the nationalised industries, notwithstanding any changes planned in the size of the public sector. The Government's own proposals for a new comprehensive legislative framework makes the case for a corresponding comprehensive parliamentary monitoring arrangement through the committees of the House irrefutable. Alternatively, the House could give renewed consideration to the proposals put forward in the 1983 Parliamentary Control of Expenditure (Reform) Bill for extending the remit of the Committee of Public Accounts to include the Value for Money Examination of the nationalised industries. Given the authority to form a sub-committee for this purpose, the PAC could well prove to be both the most appropriate and, to all concerned, the most acceptable body to provide parliamentary scrutiny.

To ensure that committee reports on Estimates have a reasonable chance of being debated on the floor of the House, the number of Estimate Days should be increased to something like the eight days recommended by the Select Committee on Procedure (Supply) 1981, and they should be reserved for debates on the basis of reports from the departmental select committees. Annual debating opportunities are already available for reports from the PAC, and Estimate Days should only be used for debating their reports in exceptional circumstances. Half of the time during the first 6 Estimate Days was devoted to reports from the PAC. The limited opportunities available at present for debating select committee reports on financial matters discourages committees from spending their time on such inquiries. There is also a need to enforce rigorously as far as possible the 'rule of relevance' from the Chair to ensure that the experience of earlier Supply Days (general political debates taking the place of a debate on the grant in question) is not repeated.

The committees themselves need to introduce a number of changes in their approach to their tasks; some are contingent on the procedural changes suggested above, others are not.

As discussed in the previous chapters, the departmental select committees so far have not regarded the monitoring of departmental expenditure as their main duty. Their choice of priorities, though perfectly consistent with their term of reference, nonetheless defeated some of the objectives of the 1979 reforms. The House is unquestionably better equipped to scrutinize the formulation of Government policies in 1985 than it was ten years earlier, and the public is better informed about the variety of complex issues involved. It would be difficult to claim the same about financial matters. Some improvements have been made but the "more effective control and stewardship" [3] envisaged in 1978 has been largely achieved in other than financial areas.

There is considerable 'expertise' in financial matters on the backbenches which has not yet been put to use in the select committees of the House. Almost half of the backbenchers in the 1983 Parliament described their occupation as businessmen or company directors and there were more qualified accountants among them than in some of the major Government Departments. There were apparently 19 qualified accountants in the House in 1982 [4] 11 at the Home Office, 1 at the Foreign Office, [5] and only 4 qualified accountants at the Audit Branch of the Treasury [6]. The House is thus not ill-equipped to tackle financial issues during the examination of the departments, and given the opportunity and encouragement to do so, all select committees should be able to set up a finance sub-committee and man it with Members willing and able to consider such questions.

There is no contradiction between this proposal and the findings of the interviews with Members described in Chapter 4. The interviews were conducted with the most active, long-term members and since the committees have so far, concentrated their attention on policy issues, active members were naturally those whose interests were in these areas. The Treasury & Civil Service Committee succeeded in achieving the highest attendance rate for Members between 1979-83, though this was the committee which paid the most attention to monitoring expenditure.

The committees should make greater use of their unrestricted opportunities to appoint external advisers for particular financial inquiries. There are retired senior civil servants, well versed in the intricacies of departmental finances whose expertise could be called on more frequently by select committees. Such advisers could be invaluable for inquiries into departmental administration, or for interpreting the information becoming available as a result of the FMI.

There is a need for the committees to make a realistic assessment of the likely impact of their inquiries. The greater publicity which surrounds the examination of ministerial witnesses does not necessarily indicate the actual impact of an inquiry, nor the extent to which a committee's recommendations are accepted and implemented. Ministers are not likely to volunteer new information if they can help it during committee inquiries and additional information is much more likely to become available from witnesses from the departments, than from ministers. It will be civil servants in Whitehall who will make serious attempts to implement recommendations since they are well aware of the possibility of being reexamined by committees in the years to come. Senior civil servants usually stay in their posts considerably longer than ministers thus are more likely to have to answer 'follow-up' questions later one. The importance of the need for making such questions a regular part of the programme of all committees cannot be overemphasised.

In their latest report, [7] the Liaison Committee stated that the consideration of the Main Estimates "... can be absorbed without too great difficulty in the working pattern of the select committees concerned..." It is for the committees to ensure, that this does in fact take place.

The responsibility of the departmental select committees is considerable. The new, extended committee system virtually exhausts all available backbencher time for detailed monitoring. Issues which escape the select committees' attention are unlikely to receive detailed scrutiny by Parliament altogether. Although their 'permissive' terms of reference allows the committees to chose their priorities in accordance with their own interests some tasks need performing if they are to be carried out by Parliament at all. The examination of government expenditure on a 'systematic basis' is unquestionably the most important among these.

Hence all committees would be well advised to allocate the necessary time for the consideration of both Main and Supplementary Estimates and PE plans on a regular basis, and use specialist assistance more freely in their examinations. Follow-up questions from previous years should be a regular part of such inquiries, as indeed for any others. If the committees were given the right to form financial sub-committees on an ad hoc basis, their programme in other respects would not be disrupted. However, if no such opportunities were to be provided, there would be a need for the committees to re-assess their priorities and to devote more of their attention to financial matters, and to departmental administration. Such re-assessment might well lead to somewhat less emphasis on the consideration of policy proposals in the future, but this is a price they should be willing to pay if effective monitoring of public expenditure is to be carried out through the committees of the House.

One further alternative can be considered. The membership of the departmental select committees could be reduced to allow the House to set up a new Select Committee on the Estimates with terms of reference to consider all Supplementary Estimates and such aspects of the Main Estimates as they deem appropriate. Adequately staffed, even if not on a scale comparable to the support available to the PAC, an Estimates Committee could provide the House with the necessary information for more effective debates on the Estimates on a continuous basis.

The departmental committees could continue to carry out the types of inquiries on the basis of which they have already established their considerable reputation, and refer to the new Estimates Committee any questions arising in connection with the Estimates during the course of their inquiries. The reduced membership would hardly affect their operation since, in practice, attendance in general is around 75% in any case and many regard smaller groups as more effective for the examination of witnesses.

Yet another select committee reform, such as the one proposed here, though is not likely to recommend itself at present. However, if the present system appears to leave too many questions unanswered the possibility of further changes cannot be excluded, and a new Estimate Committee could be one option.

NOTES

[1]   1R Procedure Committee 1977-78. op. cit. Appendix
       38.
[2]   D. Englefield et al. op. cit. p. 122.
[3]   1R Proc. Cttee 1977-78. op. cit. p.viii.
[4]   Compiled from The Times Guide to the House of
       Commons 1983.
[5]   Financial Times 18 June 1984.
[6]   Evidence Submitted by the Treasury to the Committee
       of Public Accounts 11.10.1982.
[7]   1R Liaison Committee 1984-85 HC. 363. 1c. iv.

64

9 Conclusions

The 1979 select committee reforms have led to a number of important and irreversible changes, though in some respects the new committee system has not yet lived up to expectations.

The House and the public are now considerably better informed about a great variety of subjects and in the future few policy decisions are likely to escape critical, detailed scrutiny from the select committees of the House. Comments from select committees have become an important factor to be taken into consideration when putting forward policy proposals. By providing the House with a more formalised system for expressing detailed comments, the committee reform unquestionably contributed towards redressing the balance of power between the Executive and the Legislature.

For individual MPs the committees provide opportunities for getting detailed knowledge about some aspects of Government activities, enabling them to make better informed contributions to debates; and also giving them the chance to 'examine' ministers, senior civil servants and a very wide range of experts.

To the public the select committees provide increased opportunities for letting their views be known directly to Parliament on the issues under consideration; these opportunities are much used by pressure groups and by professional organisations.

The extended select committee system means extra work for Whitehall, but also provides extra opportunities to inform Parliament about their work. In a general climate described by a former Chief Secretary to the Treasury [1] as a "Them and Us" attitude between Ministers and Civil Servants, such opportunities are not to be dismissed lightly.

These achievements of the new select committees seem almost sufficient to guarantee that the new system will be able to operate for the benefit of all concerned for some time to come. Almost, but not quite. In one important aspect, the committees have not fulfilled expectations so far. The scrutiny of public expenditure by the House has been neither more regular, nor noticeably more effective than previously, as a result of the new committees' work over the first 5 years. Opportunities have now been increased to allow the committees a formal role in the consideration of the Estimates and the committees should regard it of paramount importance to utilize these opportunities fully. The House never forgets for long its traditional role of controlling the purse strings even if the degree of enthusiasm for the necessary work involved fluctuates. Nor is the House averse to procedural reforms, when its select committees appear to overlook some of their tasks. Previous select committees, such as the specialist committees of the 1960s, and the Expenditure Committee, have been the victims of the reforming zeal of the House.

Control of public expenditure is a perennial subject of parliamentary debates in general terms; its importance is being exalted equally by those who believe in reducing the total and by those who would wish to see it increased. Both sides look to the now comprehensive select committee system of the House to provide the detailed information necessary for supporting their case. All MPs subscribe to the principle that the select committees are the appropriate agencies for carrying out this task for Parliament, even though few are actually willing to take part in the work involved. If the House is not content that the monitoring of public expenditure is carried out by the departmental select committees adequately, there is some risk that yet again some major and perhaps undesirable changes in procedure will be contemplated which would endanger much of what the new committees have already achieved.

A regular, systematic involvement in the examination of public expenditure would be a major factor in assuring the survival of the new committee system and its development to its full potential. It is perhaps worth remembering that the senior select committee of the House, the Committee of Public Accounts, which has been in existence for over a century, owes both its high reputation and continued survival to its contribution to the parliamentary control of public expenditure.

A reincarnated Bagehot would perhaps still be able to note the tendency to profilgacy in the House of Commons, but he would be the first to acknowledge that opportunities for the House to exercise financial control have increased greatly. He might even conclude that the House is no longer unconcerned with economies; but he would need some convincing that such concerns were among the major preoccupations of the House.

NOTES

[1]   Barnett, Joel Inside the Treasury, Andree Deutsch 1982. p. 188.

Selected bibliography

Books and Articles

Abramowitz, M & Eliasberg, V : The Growth of Public Expenditure in Great Britain NBER 1957

Bagehot, W The English Constitution 11th Impression, Fontana 1975

Barnett, J Inside the Treasury Andree Deutsch 1982

Butler, D and Solman, A British Political Facts 1900-1975 Macmillan, 1975

Davies, A Reformed Select Committees : The First Year The Outer Circle Policy Unit 1980

Diamon, Lord Public Expenditure in Practice George Allen & Unwin 1975

Einzig, P The Control of the Purse Secker & Warburg 1959

Englefield, D (ed) Commons Select Committees; Catalysts for Progress Longmann 1984

Flegmann, V Called to Account Gower 1980

Flegmann, V Government Departments and Select Committees of the House of Commons Paper to the Political Studies Association Annual Conference, Hull 1981

Flegmann, V Focus on Policy Issues in the Work of the Departmental Select Committees of the House of Commons, paper to the European Consortium for Political Research Conference, Freiburg, 1983

Hailsham, Lord The Dilemma of Democracy, Collins 1978

May, Erskine Parliamentary Practice 19th Edition, Butterworth 1976 20th Edition, Butterworth 1983

OECD Economic Survey, United Kingdom 1985

Peacock, A The Political Economy of Public Spending Mercantile Credit Lecture, University of Reading 1971

Robinson, A Parliament and Public Spending, Heinemann 1978

Times Guide to the House of Commons 1979

Times Guide to the House of Commons 1983

Parliamentary Papers

Reports from the Departmental Select Committees
Government Replies to Committee Reports
Hansard Reports on Parliamentary Debates
1R Select Committee on Procedure 1968-69. HC.410
1R Select Committee on Procedure 1977-78. HC.588
1R Select Committee on Procedure (Supply) 1980-81. HC.118
1R Select Committee on Procedure (Finance) 1982-83. HC.24
11R Expenditure Committee 1976-77 HC.535
1R Liaison Committee 1982-83. HC.92
1R Liaison Committee 1984-85. HC.363
'Machinery of Government' (Haldene Report) Cd. 9230
'Control of Public Expenditure' (Plowden Report) Cmnd. 1432
'Efficiency and Effectiveness in the Civil Service' Cmnd. 8616
'Financial Management in Government Departments' Cmnd. 9058

Index

Erratum
The page numbers given in the index are incorrect.
For pages from 17 to 37 add two numbers, for pages from 38 to 66, add four numbers